GROW YOUR MIND

FACE
YOUR
FEARS

Written by Alice Harman
Illustrated by David Broadbent

CRABTREE
PUBLISHING COMPANY
WWW.CRABTREEBOOKS.COM

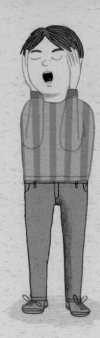

CRABTREE
PUBLISHING COMPANY
WWW.CRABTREEBOOKS.COM

Author: Alice Harman
Series designer: David Broadbent
Illustrator: David Broadbent
Editor: Crystal Sikkens
Proofreader: Melissa Boyce
Print coordinator: Katherine Berti

A trusted adult is a person (over 18 years old) in a child's life who makes them feel safe, comfortable, and supported. It might be a parent, teacher, family friend, social worker, or another adult.

Library and Archives Canada Cataloguing in Publication

Title: Face your fears / written by Alice Harman ; illustrated by David Broadbent.
Names: Harman, Alice, author. | Broadbent, David, 1977- illustrator.
Description: Series statement: Grow your mind | Includes index. | First published in Great Britain in 2020 by the Watts Publishing Group.
Identifiers: Canadiana (print) 20200221930 |
   Canadiana (ebook) 20200222007 |
   ISBN 9780778781691 (hardcover) |
   ISBN 9780778781776 (softcover) |
   ISBN 9781427125958 (HTML)
Subjects: LCSH: Courage in children—Juvenile literature. | LCSH: Fear in children—Juvenile literature. | LCSH: Worry in children— Juvenile literature. | LCSH: Anxiety in children—Juvenile literature. | LCSH: Courage—Juvenile literature. | LCSH: Fear—Juvenile literature. | LCSH: Worry— Juvenile literature. | LCSH: Anxiety—Juvenile literature.
Classification: LCC BF723.C694 H37 2021 | DDC j179/.6—dc23

Library of Congress Cataloging-in-Publication Data

Names: Harman, Alice, author. | Broadbent, David, 1977- illustrator.
Title: Face your fears / written by Alice Harman ; illustrated by David Broadbent.
   Description: New York : Crabtree Publishing Company, 2021. | Series: Grow your mind | Includes index.
Identifiers: LCCN 2020015532 (print) |
   LCCN 2020015533 (ebook) |
   ISBN 9780778781691 (hardcover) |
   ISBN 9780778781776 (paperback) |
   ISBN 9781427125958 (ebook)
Subjects: LCSH: Fear in children--Juvenile literature. | Fear--Juvenile literature.
Classification: LCC BF723.F4 H367 2021 (print) | LCC BF723.F4 (ebook) | DDC 155.4/1246--dc23
LC record available at https://lccn.loc.gov/2020015532
LC ebook record available at https://lccn.loc.gov/2020015533

Crabtree Publishing Company
www.crabtreebooks.com   1-800-387-7650
Published by Crabtree Publishing Company in 2021

Published in Canada
Crabtree Publishing
616 Welland Ave.
St. Catharines, Ontario
L2M 5V6

Published in the United States
Crabtree Publishing
347 Fifth Ave.
Suite 1402-145
New York, NY 10116

Printed in the U.S.A./082020/CG20200601

First published in Great Britain in 2020 by The Watts Publishing Group Copyright © The Watts Publishing Group 2020

CONTENTS

Fear and mindsets

Sometimes it can seem like other people don't get scared at all, like you're the only one. But that's just not true!

Everyone has to deal with fears and worries sometimes—even your strictest teacher, your loudest classmate, and your favorite celebrity.

You can't learn to never feel fear—and you shouldn't want to! Fear can sometimes help to keep us safe and make good choices.

But you can learn how best to face your fears so that they don't stop you from feeling happy and doing what you want in life.

We sometimes think of our brains as being fixed the way they are. We call this a **fixed mindset**. This way of thinking can make it feel like our fears will stay with us forever and never feel any easier to understand and manage.

But in reality, our brains are always growing and changing. Billions of **neurons** in your brain constantly pass messages to each other along connecting paths. What you think and do can build and strengthen connections that help you face your fears.

In fact, even just believing that you have the ability to learn and change is a really great start. We call this a **growth mindset**, and this book will help you to develop it.

Let's get started!

What are you afraid of?

The first step in learning how to face our fears is figuring out what they actually are! For instance, you might be scared of reading out loud in class. Think about it—why do you have this fear?

Breaking down our fears in this way helps us to see them more clearly and better understand exactly why we feel scared. Then we can start thinking about what we can do to manage our fears.

Is it that you don't like the feeling of everyone looking at you? Could that be because you're worried you'll make a mistake in front of them and they'll be mean about it or think badly of you?

Ask a trusted adult to help you create **mind maps** that break down your three biggest fears. Talk through each fear in turn. What about them makes you feel afraid?

Mind map

Let's imagine you're scared of the ocean. Why? It could be the idea of fish touching you, waves knocking you over, the ground sinking under your feet, sharks in the deep water, or something else.

What positive actions could you take to help you feel safer and more able to face this fear? Write an action plan with an adult, and check in once a week to talk about how you feel it's going.

Give it a minute

When your brain thinks that it needs to protect you from danger, a kind of "fear switch" flips inside it. This floods your body with substances, such as **adrenaline**, that make you feel like running, getting angry, or freezing on the spot. You might feel your heart pounding in your chest or a rush of cold through your body.

Your brain is trying to keep you safe by preparing your body to escape or overcome the threat, but if you're not actually in danger it's not very helpful!

If you feel this "fear switch" flip on and you start getting all panicky, just give yourself a minute to calm down. You'll then be able to think more clearly and find it easier to behave in a way that you choose, rather than acting out of fear.

Here are some ways that you could spend a minute to try to calm yourself down. Think of some of your own ideas too.

You could:

★ Take some deep **"umbrella breaths."** To do this, imagine your belly opening up like an umbrella as you breathe in, and slowly closing again as you breathe out.

★ Count slowly to 20 and then back down again. Imagine each number having a different color or pattern.

★ Sing one of your favorite songs in your head.

★ Picture all your favorite people and things, such as foods, animals, fun places, toys, or anything you like.

9

You're not alone

Sometimes you might not want to talk about your fears, maybe because you're embarrassed or because it feels too hard to say them out loud. You might also feel like you should be able to deal with your fears by yourself. But this can feel really lonely, and make your fears even worse.

Remember that your trusted adults want to help you deal with your fears, so always let them know if you're scared or worried about something.

Not all fears are ones you should learn to face, either. If you're scared because someone is hurting or bullying you, or doing things that make you feel bad or strange, that's something that just needs to stop. Tell a trusted adult so they can help keep you safe.

Alfie

When I stayed at my grandma's house, most of the time it was fine. But I was always scared about accidentally making a mess, breaking something, or being too loud because my grandma suddenly got so angry.

She'd shout really loudly in my face, grab my arm so hard that it hurt, and send me outside in the yard for a long time as punishment.

I felt too nervous to tell my dads for a while, but one day I was so scared of going that I ended up bursting into tears and telling them everything.

They were really glad I told them and said they would handle it now. They told me I did the right thing by not ignoring my scared feelings. Now I know that I can ask them for help, and that it's wrong for adults to make me feel scared.

Meet your fears

Sometimes, fears are obvious—if you think about them, you feel really scared or nervous right away. You might even feel shaky, get a stomachache, or feel sick.

But sometimes fears are hidden inside other feelings. Being scared can make us feel weak, so we may cover it up with another feeling, such as anger, without even knowing we're doing it. We might also worry that our fear is silly, and not want to admit to it.

But if something makes you feel scared, then that's all that matters. And whatever it is, there will definitely be other people who get just as scared as you about it!

With a trusted adult, make a list of things that:

★ you really don't like;

★ make you feel angry;

★ you refuse to do, and say are stupid.

For example, maybe you think playing sports is stupid. But, actually, it might be that you're scared of not doing well, so it feels better to pretend you don't care?

Talk about your lists and try to figure out whether some of the things you wrote down make you feel a bit scared or worried. Then make some mind maps to get to know these fears better, as you did in the activity on page 7.

Being brave

Being brave doesn't mean never feeling scared—that's impossible! And it doesn't mean ignoring fear either.

Bravery is about working to overcome our fears. We all have different fears, so what might be easy for one person to do, could take a huge amount of bravery for someone else.

For example, someone with no fear of heights isn't being brave when they travel in an elevator to the top floor of a tall building. But someone who is afraid of heights might need to be very brave to do that.

By facing our fears and dealing with uncomfortable feelings, we help ourselves feel more free and less afraid in the long term. That's real bravery!

Selim

My parents took me to a show at the community center down the road and it was so good! One of the groups was made up of kids around my age who played traditional music together, and my dad said I could join if I wanted.

I really wanted to, but they were so good. I was scared they wouldn't want me to join the group. The first time I tried to go to a practice, my dad walked me up to the door but then I got so scared I made him take me back home again.

I felt really bad and silly, but my dad told me it was totally natural to get scared sometimes. We practiced playing on my dad's traditional musical instruments over the weekend, then the next week I went back and we walked in together.

Everyone was really friendly and they didn't mind at all that I was a beginner. The teacher showed me some basic notes and I played along right away. I felt really proud of myself for being brave, and I love music group now!

LITTLE STEPS

Although your brain is always growing and learning, making big changes to the way you think, such as being able to manage your fears, takes a little more time and effort.

If you're scared about something and don't want to be, this might feel frustrating. You might think, "That's not fast enough, I need to stop feeling scared right now."

But give your brain a chance! You'll make progress as long as you take things step by step. Although it might feel slow and difficult at first, if you keep going you can really help change the way your brain thinks about your fears—hopefully for good.

With a trusted adult, create a step-by-step action plan to help your brain manage your fears.

First, think about what the ultimate goal of facing your fear would look like. For example, if you're afraid of the dark it might be, "I will be able to go to sleep with the lights turned off." On a piece of paper, draw a ladder with this goal at the top.

Talk with a trusted adult about what you find scary about sleeping in the dark. How could you break down your journey toward this goal into smaller steps that feel less scary?

Perhaps you could start by keeping your bedroom door open and the light on outside. Then you might close the door a little more each night until eventually you go to sleep in complete darkness. Write these actions on the steps going up the ladder, and color them in as you climb toward your goal!

Big leaps

Even when we break our fear-facing journeys down into smaller steps, there are still moments when we have to really challenge ourselves in order to make progress.

These "big leaps" forward might make us feel quite worried or scared. We can also end up thinking of them in a fixed-mindset way (see page 5), as moments where we will either succeed or fail in facing our fears.

For example, if you're nervous about sleeping anywhere that isn't your own home, going over to a friend's house for your first sleepover might feel like a "big leap." And getting too upset and needing to go home could feel like you failed. But that's not true at all!

These "big leaps" are just part of a long learning journey. It isn't important that they go perfectly, what matters is what we learn from them and how we move on with our journey.

Laura

When my friend Daisy invited me to her birthday
sleepover party, it sounded like so much fun.
The only problem was I couldn't stop worrying
about having to stay the night in a strange place.

I talked to my mom and stepdad and they were really nice. We agreed
that I would go to the party, because I didn't want to miss out, but they
would come and pick me up at any time if I wanted to go home.

I had fun at the party, but as we were going to bed I felt so
worried that I got a bad stomachache and I couldn't get to sleep. I
told Daisy's mom, and my parents came to pick me up right away.

I felt embarrassed, and it seemed like I had failed, but no one minded
at all. They were just happy I tried and I hadn't missed the
party altogether. I felt much better knowing that there
was no pressure, and at the next sleepover
I stayed the whole night!

NOW ISN'T THEN

When you have a bad experience, you might be scared about it happening again and try to avoid anything you connect to that experience.

For example, if one time you bit into an apple and ate a rotten piece, it might make you feel worried about eating an apple in the future in case it happens again. This is your brain's way of trying to protect you.

But with most apples you'll just get a lovely sweet crunch, not a horrible rotten taste. It would be a shame to never eat an apple again because of one bad experience!

If you know that something is safe, try to help your brain understand that having one bad experience doesn't mean the same thing will happen every time.

Rahim

I always used to love going to the playground to spend time with my friends, until one day I fell off the big climbing frame and really hurt myself.

Then, when we got home, I realized I lost my favorite tiger that I always keep in my pocket. My mom went back, but she couldn't find it.

I didn't want to go back to the playground ever again, even though it meant not seeing my friends there. But my mom helped me remember all the fun times I had at the playground, and I realized that having one bad time didn't mean it couldn't be fun again.

I decided to go back, but stayed on the swings at first. I made sure I emptied my pockets and gave everything to my mom before I went on them.

STORY TIME'S OVER

Our imagination is an amazing thing. It helps us create stories, games, and all kinds of other fun things. But sometimes it can also be really unhelpful— especially when it comes to our fears.

When we are scared or worried, we often tell ourselves horrible stories about what's going to happen. We might feel that just imagining these terrible things is going to make them come true—like some sort of bad magic.

We might even start doing certain actions, such as touching or counting things, to make us feel like we're stopping these bad things from happening.

It's important to talk to a trusted adult if you're having difficult feelings, so they can help you manage your worries.

Talk with a trusted adult about something that scares you. Then, write down the worst version of what you're worried might happen.

Next, write down the wildest, most out-there version you can think of—add aliens, dragons, mermaids—anything you like!

For example, maybe your "worst fear" version of having a birthday party is that no one will come. Your "wildest" version might be that it gets invaded by a pack of flying monkeys that steal all your birthday cake!

Does imagining the strange creatures in your "wildest" version mean they will appear? No! It's a story—and the "worst fear" version is too. No one can predict the future, and thinking something doesn't make it come true.

When you find your thoughts spiraling into negative, scary stories, try repeating "That's just a story" in your head or out loud. Talk with a trusted adult so they can help you too.

See the other side

When we feel really scared about something, it can be hard to ever imagine not being scared. What would that even look like?

Well, try picturing it! One really helpful way to develop a growth mindset (see page 5) is to **visualize** yourself managing your fears.

For example, if you're scared of horses you could imagine yourself happy and smiling as you stroke one on the neck.

Thinking positively about facing your fears can give you a great boost to keep on trying—even when things feel really challenging. Give it a try!

Roisin

When I started swimming lessons at school,
I didn't know what to expect and it made me
feel really nervous.

I was especially afraid of going underwater. I felt like I would never
be able to put my head below the surface. I talked to my aunt
about it and she showed me how to visualize myself swimming.

I created a picture in my mind where I was swimming
underwater beside my aunt. We were both smiling and
having a nice time together. I described it out loud to my
aunt and thought about how the water would feel, how it
would sound, and so on. This made it feel real.

The next time I went to the pool,
I felt so much more positive!
I'm making good progress and
feeling really proud of myself
for trying so hard.

INNER CRITIC

Sometimes the thing we're most scared of isn't anything like snakes or spiders. It's a voice inside our head telling us we're not good enough and we don't deserve good things to happen.

This voice can be the reason we don't want to try new challenges, and it can make us feel really bad if we don't do everything perfectly the first time.

The most important thing you can do if you're thinking these mean, untrue things about yourself is to talk to a trusted adult. Just sharing your difficult thoughts and feelings can help them fade away.

You can also try to develop a more positive growth mindset (see page 5) by thinking about your life as a journey, and reminding yourself of how many things you've already learned over the years.

Jon

Last year I was getting into a lot of trouble at school for fooling around in class and not paying attention. The school called my parents in, but I didn't want to talk about what was really wrong.

The truth was, I wasn't trying hard in class because I didn't think I was smart enough to bother. I was scared that if I made any effort, I'd find out I was right. As long as I fooled around, I could just blame it on my behavior.

My teacher talked to me about developing a growth mindset, and we tried some practice activities. I realized it was unhelpful to think of anyone as smart or not smart, and that really took the pressure off me.

Since then, I've been focusing on putting in effort and I feel so much better. The voice in my head is much nicer to me now!

Hard to hear

It can feel really scary to imagine people telling us that we've done something wrong, and it can make us act in a nervous or **defensive** way.

Sometimes people might be unfair or mean, and that's not helpful. But listening to **constructive feedback**—where someone is trying to teach you something as kindly as possible—can be really helpful for growing your brain.

By facing up to our fear of hearing anything negative about the way we've acted, we can make sure not to miss these helpful learning opportunities.

We can also teach our brain that everyone makes mistakes, but what counts is how we make it up afterward.

To start off, write down something that you are scared that someone, such as a friend, family member, or teacher, might say to you.

Talking with a trusted adult, decide whether your example is just mean or whether it is trying to be helpful. If you think it's trying to be helpful, what could you learn from it? What positive steps could you take to put this learning into action?

For example, "You're stupid" is always mean, untrue, and unhelpful. On the other hand, "You've hurt my feelings" isn't nice to hear either, but it could be a good opportunity to learn and grow.

What if I've hurt someone's feelings?

If you've hurt someone's feelings, you can think about what you've done and how you could make things right. You can try to change your behavior in the future to avoid hurting others.

KEEP FACING YOUR FEARS!

Read through these tips for a quick reminder
of how you can learn to face your fears.

Make mind maps to break down your fears
and figure out exactly what makes you feel afraid.

If you feel panicky, take a minute to do something that helps calm you down.

Always talk to a trusted adult about your fears, even if it feels difficult.

Find hidden fears by thinking about things that
make you angry or that you say are stupid.

Remember that being brave is about working
through your fears, not ignoring them.

Create a step-by-step plan to help your brain
learn to manage your fears over time.

Think of facing your fears as an ongoing journey,
not as moments where you succeed or fail.

Remember that one bad experience doesn't
mean the same thing will happen every time.

When you find yourself imagining that horrible things are going to happen,
remind yourself that it's just a story and talk to a trusted adult.

Visualize a future version of yourself managing
your fears to help you believe it's possible.

Don't listen to the mean voice in your head telling you that you're
not good enough—talk to a trusted adult about it instead.

Accept that everyone makes mistakes and
think about them as learning opportunities.

Glossary

adrenaline   A natural substance that your body produces when it thinks you are in danger

constructive feedback   When someone is trying to teach you how to do something differently, in a kind and supportive way

defensive   Feeling worried or angry about being criticized

fixed mindset   If you are using a fixed mindset, you believe that your intelligence is fixed and can't be changed

growth mindset   If you are using a growth mindset, you believe that your intelligence is always changing because your brain can grow stronger

mind map   A diagram with lines and circles for organizing information so that it is easier to remember

neurons   Cells in your brain that pass information back and forth to each another

umbrella breath   A slow, deep breath in which you imagine your belly opening and closing like an umbrella

visualize   To picture something in your mind that you would like to come true in the future

Index

Notes for adults

The concept of a "growth mindset" was developed by psychologist Carol Dweck, and is used to describe a way in which effective learners view themselves as being on a constant journey to develop their intelligence. This is supported by studies showing how our brains continue to develop throughout our lives, rather than intelligence and ability being static.

Responding with a growth mindset means being eager to learn more and seeing that making mistakes and getting feedback about how to improve are important parts of that journey.

A growth mindset is at one end of a continuum, and learners move between this and a "fixed mindset"—which is based on the belief that you're either smart or you're not.

A fixed mindset is unhelpful because it can make learners feel they need to "prove" rather than develop their intelligence. They may avoid challenges, not wanting to risk failing at anything, and this reluctance to make mistakes—and learn from them—can negatively affect the learning process.

Help children develop a growth mindset by:

• Giving specific positive feedback on their learning efforts, such as "Well done you've been practicing..." rather than non-specific praise, such as "Good effort" or comments such as "Smart girl/boy!" that can encourage fixed-mindset thinking.

• Sharing times when you have had to persevere learning something new and what helped you succeed.

• Encouraging them to keep a learning journal, where they can explore what they learn from new challenges and experiences.

• Helping them understand which fears are appropriate for them to work on managing (with trusted adults' guidance and support), and which situations—such as bullying—are not something they should have to face, and need to be handled by adults.